KT-155-275

I Love Farm Animals

By Lisa Regan

Illustrated by Kim Thompson

Miles Kelly

First published in 2008 by Miles Kelly Publishing Ltd
Harding's Barn, Bardfield End Green,
Thaxted, Essex, CM6 3PX, UK

Copyright © Miles Kelly Publishing Ltd 2008

This edition printed 2011

2 4 6 8 10 9 7 5 3

Publishing Director Belinda Gallagher
Creative Director Jo Cowan
Editorial Assistant Toby Tippen
Designer Carmen Johnson
Production Manager Elizabeth Brunwin
Reprographics Stephan Davis, Ian Paulyn
Assets Lorraine King

All rights reserved. No part of this publication may be
stored in a retrieval system, or transmitted by any means,
electronic, mechanical, photocopying, recording or otherwise,
without the prior permission of the copyright holder.

ISBN 978-1-84810-041-1

Printed in China

ACKNOWLEDGEMENTS
Page 12 Anjark/Fotolia.com; 19 Eric Isselée/Fotolia.com;
22 Nicolette Neish/Fotolia.com
All other images from the Miles Kelly Archives

British Library Cataloguing-in-Publication Data
A catalogue record for this book is available
from the British Library

Made with paper from a sustainable forest

www.mileskelly.net   info@mileskelly.net

www.factsforprojects.com

Contents

Chickens

Female chickens are called hens. Male chickens are called cockerels or roosters. A hen's babies hatch from eggs and are called chicks. Not all eggs hatch. Some are collected and sent to the shops for us to buy and eat. People may eat the meat from chickens, too.

Chicks are born with bright-yellow feathers. They follow their mother wherever she goes.

Overnight, chickens are kept in a wooden hut to protect them from hungry foxes that may creep onto the farm.

The red part on top of a hen's or rooster's head is called the comb.

Making noise

A rooster usually has a long tail and bright colours on its head. It makes a crowing noise that sounds like 'cock-a-doodle-doo'.

Cows

A group of cows is called a herd. Every day, the farmer uses a machine to milk the herd. It is important that there is lots of grass for cows to eat, as this helps them to make milk. A cow usually has one baby every year, which is called a calf.

These pale-brown cows are called Jersey cows.

Good for you

Milk is the basic ingredient for dairy foods such as yoghurt, cheese and butter. They help you grow bigger and stronger with healthy bones.

Cows chew and swallow grass, then bring it back into their mouths as cud. They can chew cud for up to eight hours each day!

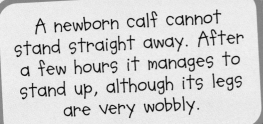

A newborn calf cannot stand straight away. After a few hours it manages to stand up, although its legs are very wobbly.

A cow's tail can swish from side to side to flick away flies and insects that try to bite.

Sheep

A baby sheep is called a lamb. Female sheep give birth to one, two or three babies each year. The mother feeds her babies on milk, which helps them to grow strong and healthy. Sheep usually live in a big group called a flock.

The name for a female sheep is a ewe. A male sheep is called a ram.

A sheep has no teeth at the top of its mouth. It uses its bottom teeth and a hard pad at the top of its mouth to nibble on grass.

If you listen to a sheep calling, it sounds like it is saying 'baa'. Lambs make a squeaky noise called bleating.

Sheep grow thick coats to keep them warm in winter. A farmer may cut off the coat in summer so it can be made into knitting wool.

Watch out!
Some rams have quite large horns. They use them for fighting, usually against other rams.

Piglets

Baby pigs are called piglets. They have long snouts that they use to sniff out food. When they are born, piglets feed on their mother's milk. As they get bigger, they will eat almost anything, but the farmer gives them corn and special food pellets, too.

Pigs have hairy skin. The hairs are tough and bristly and can be used to make brushes.

Four of an adult pig's front teeth grow long and sharp. They are called tusks.

The tail is short and wiry. It can be curly, like a spring, straight, or slightly bent.

Feeding time

A female pig usually gives birth to 8 to 12 piglets. They may all try to feed from her at the same time!

Farmers keep pigs for their meat, which is called pork. Ham, bacon and sausages come from pigs as well.

Goat

Goats are hardy animals. This means they can live in places that other farm animals might find difficult, such as steep hillsides. A female goat is called a nanny, a male is called a billy and a baby is called a kid.

Goats provide milk to drink or to make cheese, and they can also be eaten as meat.

Most goats have horns, especially billy goats. Some nanny goats have horns, too.

wide-eyed

The black dot in the middle of your eye is called the pupil. It is a small hole that lets in light. A goat has long, thin pupils like slits.

Wool made from goat fur is soft and fluffy. It is cut off twice a year to make mohair and cashmere wool.

Goats are friendly and nosey. They love to follow people to find out if they have anything to eat.

Sheepdog

Dogs can be trained to help a farmer control his flock of sheep. The farmer shouts and whistles to tell the dog where to go. After a dog is trained, it obeys all the farmer's commands. Guiding them in the right direction, the sheepdog protects the sheep from danger.

The sheep all run together with the dog behind them.

This black-and-white dog is a Border Collie. It is one of the cleverest types of dog.

Sheepdogs love to run and jump. If they don't get enough exercise they may start to misbehave.

All sorts
There are different types, or breeds, of sheepdog. This long-haired breed is an Old English Sheepdog.

Goose

A goose is a type of bird. This goose is hissing to scare someone or something away. On some farms, geese are kept as guard dogs, as they honk loudly if anything comes too near. These birds prefer to wander freely and spend most of their time grazing on grass.

Goslings

Baby geese are called goslings. They hatch from eggs that are much larger than hens' eggs.

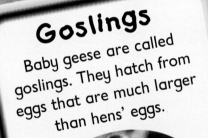

Webbed feet help geese to swim through water and glide on the surface when they land.

A goose's beak is quite sharp with a jagged edge. Some geese will nibble gently at food from a person's hand.

Soft feathers underneath a goose are called 'down'. They are sometimes used to make pillows and duvets.

The farmer feeds his geese with a mixture of grain, such as wheat, oats and barley.

Donkey

Because they are so strong and tough, donkeys can do many jobs. They can carry heavy loads, pull machinery and transport people from place to place. A donkey can walk for hours without getting tired. Donkeys are part of the same family as horses and zebras.

Because its coat isn't waterproof, a donkey needs to shelter from the rain. Donkeys usually have grey or brown fur.

It is important that a donkey's teeth are carefully checked every year by a vet, to make sure they are strong and healthy.

Carry on!
In some countries, donkeys are still used to carry heavy loads, such as food supplies.

Like horses and ponies, donkeys are measured in 'hands'. Most donkeys are under 14 hands high.

Ducks

Many ducks are found living on farms.
Sometimes the ducks are kept just as pets.
Farmers who keep ducks to sell for meat
or eggs have to look after them very
carefully. It is important that they are
fed the right kind of food.

The top layer of
feathers is covered
with an oily substance
that makes water
trickle straight off.

Heavy ducks

Some farm ducks have
white feathers and orange
beaks. These are
pekin ducks. They
are bred for meat
and eggs and
are too
heavy
to fly.

The female is called a
hen and is a speckled
brown colour all over.

A duck uses its beak, or bill, to clean its feathers. This is called preening. The beak is also used to find food.

The male is called a drake and has green feathers on his head and different colours on his body.

Ducks spend a lot of time in water. Their feet are webbed to help them swim more easily.

Horse

Horses such as the Suffolk Punch used to pull ploughs and farm machinery. This breed of horse is one of the biggest and strongest in the world. Today, horses are still kept on farms, but machines such as tractors carry out the hard work.

The long tail needs to be kept clean and brushed.

Horse plough

Horses can still been seen ploughing in competitions at country fairs.

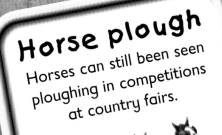

A Suffolk Punch's legs are short compared to its big, strong body.

The coat of this Suffolk Punch is a brown colour called 'chestnut'.

Most horses are kept in stables divided into small rooms called stalls. Suffolk horses live in a large yard without stalls.

Fun facts

Sheep Cutting off a sheep's woolly coat is called shearing.

Cows A cow has four different parts to its stomach that help it to digest grass.

Piglets Pigs like to roll in mud to keep cool. The mud stops their skin getting sunburnt, and keeps biting insects away.

Goats These farm animals are able to jump, climb and run and can also stand up on their two back legs.

Sheepdogs Competitions for sheepdogs are called trials. Farmers compete with their dogs to see which dog is best at moving, stopping and guiding sheep.

Geese A group of geese is called a gaggle – unless the geese are flying then the group is called a skein (say 'skayn').

Donkeys If donkeys live in a field of sheep, cows or goats, they will protect them from predators such as foxes.

Ducks Baby ducks are called ducklings. They follow their mother everywhere and are able to swim almost as soon as they've hatched.

Chickens There are more chickens in the world than any other kind of bird.

Horses Because horses are no longer used for farm work, some types, such as the Suffolk Punch, are becoming rare.